COMMON CORE CLINICS

Grade 7

English Language Arts

CLINICS

Writing and Language

Common Core Clinics, English Language Arts, Writing and Language, Grade 7
OT262 / 374NA

ISBN-13: 978-0-7836-8667-7

Cover Image: © Photolink/Photolibrary

Triumph Learning® 136 Madison Avenue, 7th Floor, New York, NY 10016

© 2012 Triumph Learning, LLC
Coach is an imprint of Triumph Learning®

ALL ABOUT YOUR BOOK

COMMON CORE CLINICS will help you master important reading skills.

Each lesson has a **Learn About It** box that teaches the idea. A sample passage focuses on the skill. A **graphic organizer** shows you a reading strategy.

Each lesson has a **Try It** passage with **guided reading**.

 Higher-Order Thinking Skills

Questions that make you think further about what you read.

Apply It provides **independent practice** for reading passages, answering short-answer questions, and responding to writing prompts.

Table of Contents

Write an Opinion

Learn About It

When you write your opinion about something, you need to state your argument clearly. An **argument** is the position you take toward a subject and the facts, reasons, and details that you give for that position. At the end of your piece, **summarize** your argument.

Read the paragraph. Use the chart below to identify the writer's opinion and supporting arguments.

Community service should be a condition for graduation from high school. By meeting this requirement, students will build powerful resumes that will help them when they are ready to join the workforce. In addition, students will form relationships with community members, who could help students in the future. These benefits will help students with school and work opportunities.

Opinion	High schools should require students to perform community service.
Reason	Students will gain work experience for their resumes.
Reason	Students will build relationships with community members.
Conclusion	Work experience and community relationships gained through community service will help students with school and work opportunities.

Try It

Read the passage. Underline the sentence that states the opinion. Place a star next to each fact, detail, or reason that supports the opinion. Use the questions to help you.

The Benefits of Learning Languages

If you visit Europe, you will meet many children who can speak more than one language. These students study many languages in school, and may have learned more than one language at home. American school children should follow their lead and learn foreign languages in preschool and elementary school.

What is the writer's opinion?

While many high schools recommend that students study foreign languages, this introduction comes too late. The brains of young children up to about seven years of age are programmed to learn language. At this point in a child's life, the brain develops according to input from the outside world; language is part of this input. Indeed, a child up until the age of three years old is better able to *hear* the individual sounds in languages. Being able to distinguish the different sounds of the language helps language learners reproduce those sounds as they speak. For this reason, people over the age of thirteen who learn a new language will almost invariably speak it with an accent. That's true even if someone over thirteen moves to a country where they are surrounded by people speaking the new language. On the other hand, children who learn languages from native speakers as infants and toddlers will retain the ability to reproduce those sounds, especially if they have consistent exposure to the language as they grow. Still, while there is a window of opportunity for learning languages between the ages of 0 to 7, there seems to be another window for children between about ten and thirteen years old. This means that even if children have not learned a second language in early childhood, there is good reason to add language classes to elementary and middle school.

What reasons support his or her opinion?

The ability to speak more than one language produces many benefits for children. Multilingual children have the capacity to think more effectively and creatively than their single-language counterparts. Their critical thinking and problem solving skills are also improved. This problem solving ability is important in mathematics. Studies have shown that children who speak more than one language actually outperform their single-language peers in mathematics. Also, people who speak more than one language have an easier time learning yet another language, if they want or need to in the future. Surprisingly, studies have even shown benefits far later in life.

What evidence about thinking skills does the writer give to support his or her argument?

Continued on the next page ➤

Continued from the previous page

It seems that the onset of Alzheimer's disease—a disease that causes loss of memory and eventually the loss of an individual's ability to function—may be delayed for those who speak more than one language.

Additionally, children who speak more than one language have expanded opportunities to pursue business relationships and careers throughout the world. In our increasingly global society, these benefits could prove substantial.

How does the writer try to persuade the reader to agree with his or her opinion?

By encouraging children to learn multiple languages at a young age, we can help give them the best possible start in life, and this start can have multiple benefits throughout their lives.

Did you come away convinced that the writer's opinion is correct? Why or why not?

Read the writing prompt. Plan your response in the graphic organizer.

PROMPT

As school budgets tighten, math and reading are prioritized, while physical education, music, and art all have been cut or reduced. If you were planning a school's schedule, which of these classes would you try to keep? Why do you think the subject is valuable?

Opinion	
Reason	
Reason	
Reason	
Conclusion	

Write your response on the lines below.

Write an Informative Piece

Learn About It

An **informative piece** tells about a topic. When you write something that informs the reader, you need to include facts, concepts, definitions, and details, and present your information clearly. Decide on an **organizational pattern**, such as chronological order, cause and effect, or compare and contrast. **Text features**, such as headings, charts, or illustrations, may help readers understand the information and organization. At the end of your piece, include a **conclusion** that supports the information you have presented.

Read the paragraph. Use the chart below to identify the heading, facts, organization, and conclusion that tell more about the topic.

Adam Clayton Powell Jr.: Civil Rights Leader

Adam Clayton Powell Jr., born in 1908, was the son of Adam Clayton Powell Sr., who was a pastor in Harlem. During the 1930s, Powell led protests that helped African Americans in New York City gain employment. Elected to Congress in 1945, he helped get important social legislation passed, but he was frequently absent. He was defeated by Charles Rangel for re-election in 1970, and died in 1972. Today, Powell is remembered both for his fighting spirit and his flaws.

Topic	Adam Clayton Powell Jr.
Organization	Chronological order
First detail	Powell was born in 1908
Second detail	Civil rights leader during Depression
Third detail	Elected to Congress in 1945
Fourth detail	Defeated in 1970
Fifth detail	Died in 1972
Conclusion	Remembered for fighting spirit and flaws

Try It

Read the passage. Underline the sentences that show the organization. Place a star next to facts, details, and definitions. Use the questions to help you.

Lucretia Coffin Mott

Lucretia Coffin Mott was a civil rights activist before the label existed. Mott was born Lucretia Coffin in Nantucket, Massachusetts, in 1793. She married James Mott in 1812. Then in 1821, she became a minister of the Religious Society of Friends, commonly called "Quakers." As a Quaker, she believed in peace and equality among all human beings. Thus, she was fiercely against slavery, and would not use goods, such as cotton and sugar, that had been produced by enslaved individuals. Being a Quaker and a minister meant that Lucretia Coffin Mott had more freedom and influence than most American women of the time.

> What topic is the writer covering?

Because United States antislavery organizations were reluctant to admit women as members, Mott helped organize women's abolitionist societies and was a founding member of the Philadelphia Female Antislavery Society. Mott was also a highly regarded speaker against slavery. In 1840, she traveled to London as a delegate for the World's Antislavery Convention. Once she arrived, she learned that other delegates of the convention refused to have women take their seats as delegates. Even so, while there, she met another important women's rights leader, Elizabeth Cady Stanton. Their meeting helped pave the way for another important civil rights event.

> What facts, details, and definitions does the writer include?

In 1848, Mott helped to organize and lead the Women's Rights Convention at Seneca Falls, New York. At this notable event, women's rights leaders such as Elizabeth Cady Stanton and Mott's sister, Martha Coffin Wright, came together to pass the *Declaration of Sentiments*, which echoed the *Declaration of Independence*, stating: *"We hold these truths to be self-evident: that all men and women are created equal…"* This simple statement could seem radical at a time when women could not vote, could not own property, and had few legal rights. Several amendments addressing women's rights were also passed, including one that stated that women should have the right to vote. Lucretia Coffin Mott was the first person to sign the document.

> What causes did Mott work for during her lifetime?

Soon after, in 1850, Mott published her book, *Discourse on Women,* about the restrictions women faced in the United States and in Western Europe. Mott wrote that women needed to have equality in legal, political, and economic matters.

Continued on the next page ➡

Continued from the previous page

Throughout these years, Mott continued to protest slavery. She and her husband opened their home to escaping slaves on the Underground Railroad. Once the Civil War ended slavery in the United States in 1865, Mott pushed for voting rights for both African Americans and women. There was infighting among her colleagues about which group should take priority in getting the vote: white women or African American men. Mott believed that all American women and men should have the right to vote, and she encouraged those arguing to see this point of view. She died in 1880.

> **What kind of organization does the writer use to present information about Lucretia Coffin Mott?**

What details from the passage support the idea that Lucretia Coffin Mott was an influential American?

Apply It

Read the writing prompt. Plan your response in the graphic organizer.

PROMPT

Choose a person from history. Find out facts and details about the person, including what makes him or her important. Then write to tell others what you have learned about this person.

Topic	
Organization	
First detail	
Second detail	
Third detail	
Fourth detail	
Fifth detail	
Conclusion	

Write your response on the lines below.

_____

_____

_____

_____

_____

_____

_____

_____

_____

_____

_____

_____

_____

_____

_____

Write a Narrative

Learn About It

When you write a **narrative**, you tell a story. Whether you are telling a true story or whether you are making up a story, you will have a beginning, middle, and end. You will also have **characters**—the people in the story. First you set up the situation, explaining the context for the story, and establish the **setting**. As the story continues, one or more characters face **conflict**—that is, they have problems. The story revolves around how the problem is resolved. The **resolution** is the conclusion of the story.

Read the passage. Look at the characters in the story. What problem does the main character face? Use the chart to help you identify parts of the story.

Ryan had saved for months to buy a new bicycle. Finally, the day came when he had enough money. Running down to the store, Ryan stopped in shock. His best friend José was wheeling the bicycle outside. José grinned.

"Hey, Ryan. How do you like my new bike?"

Situation	A boy is ready to buy a new bike.
Characters	Ryan, José
Setting	Bike store
Problem	Ryan's best friend buys the bike.
Conclusion	Will Ryan try to buy the bicycle from José? Will José offer to trade it for another bicycle when he sees how much Ryan wants it?

Try It

Read the passage. Underline the names of the characters. Pay attention to the sequence of events. Use the questions to help you.

A Hike in Tucson

When Maria and Cara visited their cousin Joaquin in Tucson, they were completely charmed by the landscape.

"Look at this saguaro cactus!" said Maria. "This must be 30 feet tall!"

"I know!" said Cara. "They're sticking up on the hill like candles on a birthday cake."

Who are the main characters?

Maria and Cara explained to Joaquin that they would love to take a hike and get a closer look at the plants and animals in his hometown.

"There's a great trail that starts just behind this block," he explained. "Just make sure you bring water. Tell someone where you're going, too. It's safer that way."

So the next morning, Cara and Maria told their Uncle Theo that they were going to take a hike. He told them about a good safe hike nearby, and they were glad to get started. It was May, and some of the succulent plants and cacti were beginning to blossom.

"Cara, look!" said Maria. "Check out that lizard!"

"Nice," said Cara. "But which trail do we take from here?" The girls had walked about a half mile, but the city block seemed far away. The trail led up a hill, and switched back and forth so that the walk wouldn't be so steep. But that meant the girls had lost track of where they were.

What is the characters' situation?

"Let's try this trail," said Maria. "It looks like more people have walked on it recently."

"Okay," agreed Cara, but she wasn't at all sure that Maria was right. As they turned up the trail, the sun began to beat down and the girls started to get hot and cranky.

"I knew this trail wasn't right," snapped Cara, after they had been walking another twenty minutes.

"Well, why didn't you say so, then?" said Maria, obviously annoyed at her sister.

Cara had nothing to say to that, so she focused on worrying about what could happen to them on the hot desert trail.

What problem do the characters face?

"Maria, did you bring any water?" asked Cara.

"Um, no. Did you?" asked Maria.

"No, I thought we would only be gone for a few minutes," said Cara.

"Don't panic, Cara. We can always call Joaquin. He can bring us water if we need it."

Continued on the next page ➤

Continued from the previous page

Cara stuck her hand in one of her pants pockets and then the other. "Maria," she asked in a whisper. "Did you bring your cell phone?"

Maria checked her pockets and knapsack. "Oh no!" she cried. "We don't have water or a cell phone? We could really be in trouble!"

"I know," said Cara. "It's getting close to noon, and the sun will be out for hours. I'm hungry and thirsty already, and I don't know where we are. What if we lose our strength out here?"

Now Maria had nothing to say. The two kept walking, hoping that, somehow, something would start to look familiar. Suddenly they heard a loud clump, clump behind them.

"Aaaa!" screamed Cara, sure they were about to get robbed.

"Calm down," said a familiar voice. The two girls rushed forward. It was Joaquin!

How is the problem resolved?

"We're so glad to see you!" said Maria.

"When you didn't come back, I got worried," he said. "I tried to call you, but then I heard your phones ringing back at the house. It's a good thing you told me where you were headed!" he cried.

"That's for sure," said Maria. "Next time I'm bringing a bottle of water, a phone, and a map. Oh, and I'm bringing you, too, Joaquin."

How does the author convey that Maria and Cara genuinely learned something?

Apply It

Read the writing prompt. Plan your response in the graphic organizer.

PROMPT

Write about a child your age who is having a problem. Use ideas from your own life or make up the story completely. Be sure to have one event lead to the next, and have a beginning, middle, and end.

Situation	
Characters	
Setting	
Problem	
Resolution	

Write your response on the lines below.

Phrases and Clauses

Learn About It

Some sentences include different types of phrases and clauses. An **introductory phrase** is at the beginning of a sentence. Use a comma if an introductory phrase uses more than four words. An **appositive** is a word or phrase set off by commas that explains the noun or pronoun that it follows. An **independent clause** has a noun and a verb, and can stand alone as a sentence. A **dependent clause** also has a subject and a verb but cannot stand alone as a sentence. Dependent clauses often start with words like *after, although,* or *if.*

Read the paragraph. Use the chart below to help you identify introductory phrases, appositives, independent clauses, and dependent clauses.

During all my years at school, my favorite days were field trips. My best friend, Joe, and I always sat together on the bus. Even if we were exhausted, we always had fun on field trips.

Sentence Part	Example
Introductory phrase	**During our trip to the city**, I learned about art.
Appositive	Our destination, **the Museum of Modern Art**, was amazing.
Independent clause	**I went with my classmates**, and my mother went, too.
Dependent clause	We were the first ones to board the bus home, **although I could barely stand to leave**.

Try It

Read the passage. Underline introductory phrases, circle appositives, and make a star near dependent clauses in a complex sentence. Use the questions to help you.

Javelinas

(1) If you were to spot a javelina in the wild, you might not recognize just what you were seeing. (2) A javelina, actually a type of wild peccary, is often thought to be a pig. (3) Scientists say that javelinas are the only native pig-like creatures that can be found living in the wild here in the United States. (4) They live in Texas, Arizona, and New Mexico, as well as in parts of Central and South America. (5) While you might think that this pig-like animal would need to be near a farm's food sources, javelinas actually survive well in the desert. (6) They eat prickly pear cactus and other types of desert plants. (7) Since human beings have been sharing the desert with them, some bold javelinas will approach people who are eating. (8) The peccaries are hoping to get a snack, and they will invade campgrounds if there's food around. (9) Unfortunately, like other wild animals that become used to getting food from humans, they can quickly become a problem.

> Remember that dependent clauses often start with words such as *although* and *while*. Is there a dependent clause in the first sentences?

(10) This unusual-looking animal is smaller than a pig, and it weighs between 35 to 50 pounds. (11) It has a long snout and it is covered in thick hair. (12) Watch out for its tusks. (13) Some say the javelina got its Spanish name because its tusks are sharp like a javelin's blade, but the name actually comes from the Spanish for "wild boar."

> An appositive explains more about, or renames, the noun or pronoun that it follows. Do you see an appositive in the first paragraph?

 **Understand**

What is the difference between an introductory phrase and a dependent clause?

Apply It

Read the passage. Answer the questions on the next page.

Water Parks

(1) During the 1940s, a new recreational opportunity became available in America. (2) Vacationers now could enjoy cooling off at a water park. (3) In the decades since then, water parks have flourished, and there are more in the United States than anywhere else in the world. (4) Experts say that more than 80 million people visit water parks each year, on average.

(5) Although some stand-alone water parks boast dozens of attractions, existing amusement parks seem to be able to boost profits by adding even just a few water elements. (6) One such park, LEGOLAND® in California, lets children take part in creating rafts with the use of soft Legos®. (7) Children can then use the rafts to float down a lazy river. (8) The lazy river, a pool with a current on which visitors float on tubes, is one of the more popular attractions in water parks everywhere.

(9) Why would a "dry park" add water features? (10) Experts say that on hot days, visitors to an amusement park will stay longer if they get a chance to cool off. (11) The opportunities to splash in a pool, float on an inner tube, or slide down a gigantic waterslide offer a different experience from the rides in the rest of a park. (12) Although these attractions are not cheap to build, they are usually cheaper than constructing complex new rides that do not use water.

(13) A newer trend in water parks is the indoor park. (14) In some popular resort areas, hotels have constructed their own elaborate water attractions. (15) With these they hope to encourage families to pay for a package of entertainment. (16) Are you tempted to jump in?

Use "Water Parks" to answer the questions. Write your answers in complete sentences.

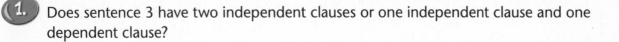

1. Does sentence 3 have two independent clauses or one independent clause and one dependent clause?

_____

_____

2. Does sentence 5 have a dependent clause? What is it?

_____

_____

3. Identify the appositive in sentence 6.

_____

_____

4. Identify the appositive in sentence 8.

_____

_____

5. Which sentence in the third paragraph starts with a dependent clause?

_____

_____

6. How would you describe sentence 14?

_____

_____

5 # Types of Sentences

Learn About It

There are different kinds of sentences. A **simple sentence** contains one independent clause made up of just one subject and one predicate. A **compound sentence** has two independent clauses joined by a conjunction or a semicolon. A **complex sentence** includes one independent clause and one or more dependent clauses. A **compound-complex sentence** includes two independent clauses joined by a conjunction or semicolon, but at least one of these independent clauses has a dependent clause.

Read the paragraph. Use the chart to help you identify simple, compound, complex, and compound-complex sentences.

As he ran for the bus, Jermaine heard his mother calling his name. He glanced over his shoulder. His mother was waving his backpack; he'd forgotten it again. Even though he knew he might miss the bus, Jermaine ran back to his mother, and he grabbed his backpack.

Sentence Type	What It Contains	Example
Simple	Subject + verb	The snake crawled out of the backpack.
Compound	Independent clause + independent clause	Campers need to stay alert; bears have been spotted in the area.
Complex	Dependent clause(s) + independent clause	Believing that nobody was listening, Felix started singing along with the radio.
Compound-Complex	Independent clause + independent clause + dependent clause(s)	The sandwich had been in the refrigerator for three weeks, and although it wasn't fit to eat anymore, it was a lovely shade of green.

Try It

Read the passage. Underline the independent clauses and circle the dependent clauses to help you identify each type of sentence. Use the questions to help you.

To Act or Not to Act

(1) Sam had no idea what he was going to do. (2) After getting a part in the school play, he had a very difficult decision to make. (3) To Sam's dismay, rehearsals for the play would be taking place at the same time as football practice. (4) Sam was the team's kicker, and he knew the team needed him. (5) He wanted to stay on the team, but he also wanted to act! (6) It wasn't fair. (7) Sam nervously walked toward his football coach's office.

Is sentence 2 compound or complex? Can each clause stand alone as a simple sentence?

(8) "Hi, Coach," Sam said as he entered the office. (9) "I have a problem. (10) I was cast in the school play, but rehearsals conflict with football practice. (11) What should I do?"

(12) "Congratulations!" Coach said. (13) He shook Sam's hand. (14) Sam stood there bewildered. (15) "I heard the competition was stiff this year (16) You know, I used to act in my school days, too. (17) Why don't I talk to your director? (18) I'm sure we can figure out a way for you to do both."

Is sentence 4 compound or complex? How many independent clauses do you see?

(19) "Thanks, Coach," Sam said. (20) He was thrilled that he could be a football player *and* an actor. (21) As he walked to his next class, he couldn't help but smile.

HOTS Apply

What conjunction would you use if you combined sentences 13 and 14 to make a compound sentence? Could you use more than one?

Apply It

Read the passage. Answer the questions on the next page.

The Speech

(1) Dawn mounted the stage slowly. (2) As she walked up the stairs near the podium, her legs trembled, and she nearly tripped in her dress-up shoes. (3) She took out the index cards containing her speech, but she fumbled them with her shaking hands. (4) "Good morning," she said—or rather, squeaked. (5) Wincing at the poor first impression she had made, she cleared her throat. (6) Her family gazed up at her with identical worried expressions. (7) Seeing them worry only made Dawn more nervous. (8) Dawn looked back down at her index cards to begin, but her voice froze in her throat.

(9) Why had she agreed to do any of this? (10) When Mr. Brown had asked her to give the keynote speech for Martin Luther King Jr. Day, Dawn had felt honored. (11) She was a talented speaker, and she greatly admired Dr. King. (12) She had eagerly jumped at the chance to make a speech about the Nobel Prize winner to her fellow students and their families.

(13) But now she was scared and anxious as she stood in front of more than 500 people. (14) She looked up again to see her older brother grin and wink. (15) Suddenly, she relaxed. (16) She had no reason to be apprehensive; she had practiced her speech many times and would do a good job. (17) With a quick look at the top card, Dawn began to speak.

Use "The Speech" to answer the questions. Write your answers in complete sentences.

1. Is sentence 1 simple, compound, or complex?

_____

_____

2. In sentence 2, how many independent clauses are there? Are there any dependent clauses?

_____

_____

3. Find a compound sentence in the passage, and write it below.

_____

_____

4. In sentence 10, what is the dependent clause?

_____

_____

5. What kind of sentence is sentence 16?

_____

_____

6. How would you describe sentence 17?

_____

_____

LESSON

6

Misplaced and Dangling Modifiers

Learn About It

A **modifier** is a word or phrase that explains more about a noun in a sentence. Many people make mistakes when using modifiers, because it is unclear what noun the modifier is explaining. A **dangling modifier** tells about a word that either is not in the sentence or does not follow logically. To correct a sentence with a dangling modifier, make sure that you include the noun that performs the action. A **misplaced modifier** is not placed closely enough to the noun that it modifies. You can correct a misplaced modifier by moving it closer to its subject.

Read the paragraph. Look for dangling and misplaced modifiers.

We almost waited an hour for our dinner to be delivered. Covered with pepperoni, the boy gobbled the pizza immediately. After dinner, tossed across the field, the same boy caught a baseball.

Modifiers	Example	Corrected Version	Reason
Misplaced	Juan and Carlos **only** saw each other during holidays.	Juan and Carlos saw each other only during holidays.	The word **only** modifies **holidays**.
Dangling	<u>At two years old, Grandfather told Bessie bedtime stories.</u>	When Bessie was two years old, Grandfather told her bedtime stories.	**Two years old** modifies **Bessie**.
Misplaced	The lunchroom staff served vegetarian "sloppy joes" to the students **on school lunch trays.**	The lunchroom staff served the students vegetarian "sloppy joes" on school lunch trays.	**On school lunch trays** modifies **sloppy joes**.

Duplicating any part of this book is prohibited by law.

Try It

Read the passage. Put a star next to any sentences that have a misplaced or dangling modifier. Use the questions to help you.

Traffic Lights

(1) Having ridden in a car, some time was spent stopped at a traffic light. (2) Without this device, bicycles, cars, and trucks, resulting in many accidents, wouldn't stop at intersections. (3) When first on the streets, this situation existed with cars. (4) At that time, bicycles, animal-powered wagons, and pedestrians also used the streets. (5) Putting in place a two-point traffic signal, traffic was monitored. (6) But significantly it did not end accidents at intersections. (7) Not offering a time interval between the "stop" and "go" positions, people still had accidents with the two-point signals. (8) It was dangerous still for people to cross intersections.

> In sentence 1, does the subject follow logically after the introductory phrase? How could you correct it?

(9) Between a car and a horse carriage an accident inspired inventor Garrett Morgan to create something that would make traffic safer—the three-point traffic signal. (10) Morgan received a patent for his device on November 20, 1923. (11) Including three commands: stop, go, and all-stop, Morgan hand-cranked the T-shaped traffic signal. (12) The all-stop halted movement in all directions, allowing pedestrians to cross the street safely.

> In sentence 2, does the phrase "resulting in many accidents" make sense where it is? Where might you move it?

(13) The influential most traffic signal ever invented is the one we use today: the electric red, yellow, and green traffic light. (14) But contributing to safety history, American traffic wouldn't have been the same without Morgan. (15) Before dying in 1963, the government of the United States recognized him for his contributions.

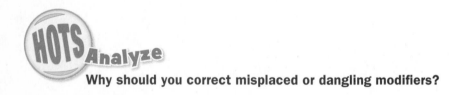

HOTS Analyze

Why should you correct misplaced or dangling modifiers?

Apply It

Read the passage. It contains mistakes. Answer the questions on the next page.

My Dog Harry

(1) At the age of six, my grandmother gave me a dog. (2) Though always slobbering, I loved the huge Great Dane. (3) I called him Harry Potter, after one of my favorite characters. (4) We entered Harry in a dog show when he was still a puppy. (5) Harry won almost the second-place prize. (6) I noticed that Harry looked quite disappointed. (7) We weren't sure we should put our fine Great Dane through that again.

(8) We all had fun playing with Harry Potter. (9) At the age of twelve, my father let me walk the dog on my own. (10) People always seemed surprised to see such a small person with such a big dog. (11) People were always impressed by my Harry. (12) Other dogs penned up in backyards would look up to admire him as we walked by.

(13) Once we thought we lost Harry Potter. (14) We found the Great Dane hiding behind a neighbor's house. (15) Frightened by a Labrador that was on the loose, we couldn't believe that Harry Potter could panic like that. (16) After hiding, we knew Harry was more nervous around strange dogs than we thought. (17) When we took him to a dog trainer, we felt like we were doing all we could for Harry. (18) A dog is, after all, a best person's friend!

Use "My Dog Harry" to answer the questions. Write your answers in complete sentences.

1. How would you rewrite sentence 1 to fix the dangling modifier?

_____

_____

2. In sentence 2, what noun does "Though always slobbering" modify? Is the sentence correct as it is?

_____

_____

3. Rewrite sentence 5 to correct the misplaced modifier.

_____

_____

4. In sentence 9, does the introductory phrase make sense with the noun that immediately follows?

_____

_____

5. Rewrite sentence 15 to correct the dangling modifier.

_____

_____

6. Rewrite sentence 18 to correct the misplaced modifier.

_____

_____

LESSON 7

Commas

Learn About It

Commas are the punctuation marks used to separate items in a list, including **coordinate adjectives**. You can recognize coordinate adjectives in two ways. First, try replacing the comma between the adjective with the word *and*. For example, if you change "the *slow-cooked, delicious* dinner" to "the slow-cooked and delicious dinner," it still sounds correct. Second, try reversing the adjectives. If you can reverse them, they are coordinate. For example, you can reverse the example to read "the delicious and slow-cooked dinner."

Read the paragraph. Look at the adjectives in the sentences, and decide where commas are needed. Then look at the chart below.

> The high-spirited frolicking children couldn't sit still in the big vegetarian restaurant. There was little that the demure restrained grandmother could do, even when other diners shot her annoyed resentful glances.

Commas	Example	Use *and* Between Adjectives	Reverse Order of Adjectives
Use commas between coordinate adjectives.	The energetic, athletic boy won first-place at the track meet.	The energetic and athletic boy won first-place at the track meet.	The athletic, energetic boy won first-place at the track meet.
Do not use commas between adjectives that are not coordinate.	Rosalina put on her gray snow boots before she went outside.	Rosalina put on her gray and snow boots before she went outside. (Not coordinate since gray modifies the whole phrase *snow boots*.)	Rosalina put on her snow, gray boots before she went outside. (doesn't follow logically)

Try It

Read the passage. As you read, underline the places that are missing the correct punctuation. Use the questions to help you.

The Climb

(1) Levi tipped back his head and looked up the rocky large mountain. (2) It was a steep difficult climb. (3) He was sorry now that he'd agreed to undertake the treacherous tiring journey. (4) Still, he'd promised his kind patient stepfather that at least he'd try. (5) His new dad was a former mountain climber and this trek up the mountain was important to him.

Remember that if adjectives are coordinate, you can use *and* between them. In sentence 2, are *steep* and *difficult* coordinate?

(6) Levi turned to where his stepfather was kneeling before their nylon backpacks. (7) He had laid out the supplies they'd brought: a flashlight, clear water bottles, snacks, and rain ponchos. (8) When he had checked each item, he gave a happy satisfied nod. (9) "That's it," he said. (10) "I think we have everything." (11) He stood and grinned jauntily at his stepson, who was a nervous inexperienced climber.

(12) "Ready, son?" the confident capable climber asked.

(13) "What about your new point-and-shoot camera?" Levi asked.

(14) "I've got it," said his stepfather.

(15) "What about your new black cell phone?" Levi asked.

Remember that coordinate adjectives can be reversed. In sentence 5, can *former* and *mountain* be reversed?

(16) "There's no reception on the mountain," his stepfather said. (17) "That's why we need all these supplies with us. (18) Ready to go?"

(19) Levi nodded. (20) "I'm right behind you," he said, with a nervous high-pitched chuckle.

HOTS Understand

How can you recognize coordinate adjectives?

Apply It

Read the passage. It contains mistakes. Then answer the questions on the next page.

Cleaning Up

(1) It was Saturday, and Tara's mother had asked her to clean her room before she went to the big school dance. (2) There were huge laundry piles. (3) Tara had old stuffed animals, schoolbooks, and various other items strewn about the bedroom floor.

(4) The impatient busy girl sighed, wishing her mother wasn't so big on cleanliness. (5) Still, it would be nice to find the new blue dress and shoes she'd mislaid sometime last week.

(6) Tara walked to the small walk-in closet, shoving a pile of dirty laundry out of the way with her foot. (7) The closet was nearly bare since most of her clothes were scattered around the bedroom. (8) The empty closet was a logical place to begin, so she decided to start her thorough organizational work there. (9) Turning on her radio, she sang along to the music as she hung her clean fragrant laundry in the closet. (10) Dirty laundry went into a large laundry basket. (11) Stray shoes went on the closet floor and books went on a long shelf. (12) Most of the stuffed animals went in a bag to be given to her younger cousin, but she did save a few for sentimental reasons.

(13) As she finished clearing the room, Cara lifted her heavy winter coat from a chair. (14) Underneath she found both the blue dress and her favorite new shoes!

Use "Cleaning Up" to answer the questions. Write your answers in complete sentences.

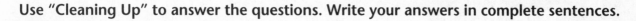

1. In sentence 1, should there be a comma between *big* and *school*? Why or why not?

_____

_____

2. In sentence 2, should there be a comma between *huge* and *laundry*? Why or why not?

_____

_____

3. Where should a comma be added in sentence 4?

_____

_____

4. In sentence 5, should there be a comma between *new* and *blue*?

_____

_____

5. Where should a comma be added in sentence 9?

_____

_____

6. In sentence 13, should there be a comma between *heavy* and *winter*? Why or why not?

_____

_____

8 Spelling

Learn About It

> **Spelling** is the order in which letters form a word. In English, there are spelling rules you can follow, though each rule sometimes has exceptions. Use a dictionary to verify the spelling of words you are not sure about.

Read the paragraph. Use the dictionary to find how to spell the highlighted words.

Mary did not realize how hard she slamed down the telephone reciever. She practically dyed of embarrassment when she realized what she had done. She was sorry that she had plaied around with the phone.

Useful Spelling Rules	Examples
Words Ending with a Single Consonant Double consonants in one-syllable words that end with a single consonant when adding -**ed** or -**ing**.	Trapped, fanning
Words Ending with -y If a word ends with a consonant and -**y**, change the -**y** to an -**i**, when adding -**ed**. Do not change the **y** when adding -**ing**. If a word ends with a vowel and -**y**, do not change the -**y** when adding -**ed** or -**ing**.	Buried, married Burying, marrying Saying, deployed
I Before E Use **i** before **e**, except after **c**, or when sounded as long **a** as in **neighbor** and **weigh**.	Piece Deceive Sleigh

Try It

Read the passage. Underline words that are misspelled. Use the questions to help you.

The Trouble with Sprawl

(1) Most cities in the United States were not planed, at least not when they began. (2) If you maped where buildings stand in many cities, especially in the East, you would discover an inner core, where buildings are close together. (3) These were (and sometimes still are) percieved to be the focal points of the urban areas. (4) Years ago, people lived, worked, and shoped in these city centers.

What word is misspelled in sentence 1?

(5) During the middle of the twentyeth century, many people left crowded cities. (6) They wanted more space, beleiving that it would make them happier. (7) Houses and shops were built on the outer perimeter of the city, farther apart from one another. (8) In the older city cores, carriing food from the store to the home wasn't a problem, since shops were in easy walking distance. (9) As suburbs became popular, however, people began buiing thier food at huge grocery stores. (10) Since stores and shops were farther from people's homes, people had to use cars to do their shoping.

Is more than one word misspelled in sentence 9?

(11) Feilds that had been farmland become valuable to developers. (12) Along with houses and stores, roads had to be constructed in these newly developed areas. (13) Of course, the farther away people moved, the more driving they had to do. (14) In time, they became more isolated, busiing themselves with maintaining their larger living spaces.

HOTS Apply

What should you do if you are not sure about a word's spelling?

Apply It

Read the passage. It contains mistakes. Answer the questions on the next page.

Going to the Chapel

(1) As soon as two people get engaged, they begin planing for thier big day. (2) Through the centuryes in the United States, many customs and traditions have grown, such as the bride and groom having close freinds and family serve as ushers and bridesmaids. (3) Some traditions have stayed the same through the years. (4) Others have changed with people's attitudes and beliefs about the right way to "tie the knot."

(5) Many young people opt for a big traditional wedding, in a religious seting. (6) The average cost of these weddings runs close to $25,000. (7) Couples may hire a wedding planer because there are so many decisions to make. (8) Some people would rather get married quickly and inexpensively. (9) For those couples, one city has created its own wedding industry. (10) Here couples can get marryed dressed as pirates or with the crew of *Star Trek*. (11) They can get an Elvis Presley impersonator to sing to them, or they can ride in a gondola. (12) Those who are really in a hurry can have a "drive-through wedding," staying in their cars. (13) This city is Las Vegas, where people have long come to have fuss-free weddings. (14) Las Vegas's wedding business grew because other cities and states made couples wait between the time they got a marriage license and the time when they could get married. (15) In Las Vegas, until recently, the Marriage Bureau staied open all night to give licenses to eager couples. (16) It still stays open until midnight.

Use "Going to the Chapel" to answer the questions. Write your answers in complete sentences.

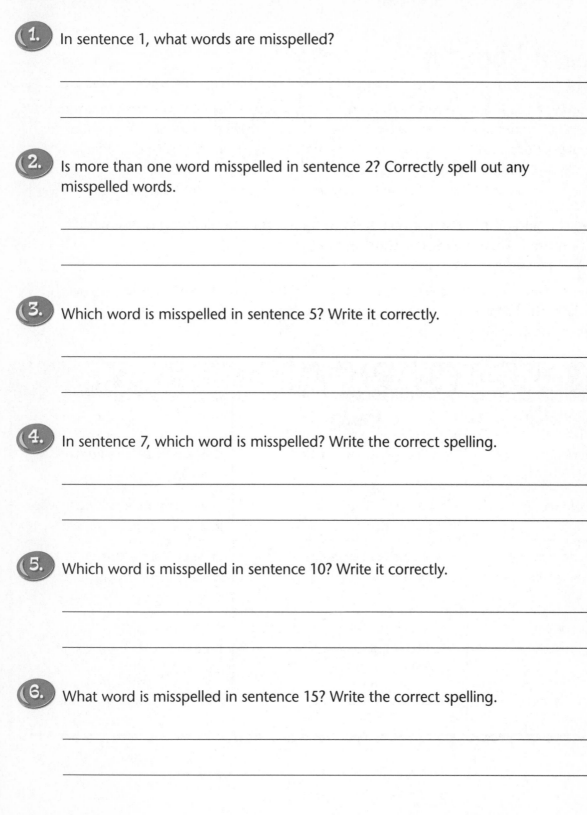

1. In sentence 1, what words are misspelled?

_____

_____

2. Is more than one word misspelled in sentence 2? Correctly spell out any misspelled words.

_____

_____

3. Which word is misspelled in sentence 5? Write it correctly.

_____

_____

4. In sentence 7, which word is misspelled? Write the correct spelling.

_____

_____

5. Which word is misspelled in sentence 10? Write it correctly.

_____

_____

6. What word is misspelled in sentence 15? Write the correct spelling.

_____

_____

Context Clues

Learn About It

Context clues are the words and sentences around or near an unfamiliar word that help you figure out what the word means. When you see an unfamiliar word, look for context clues, and then try to figure out what the word means. Use a dictionary to make sure you are correct.

Read the paragraph. Use context clues to figure out the meaning of the word *subterranean.* **Then review the chart below.**

Amaya was looking forward to visiting subterranean caverns with her science class. She had always been interested in underground rock formations and wanted to become a geologist one day.

Context Clues		
Type	**Meaning**	**Example**
Definition	Stating what a word means	Some animals are **nocturnal**: they are awake at night.
Example	Giving words that relate to the unfamiliar word	I enjoy **legumes**, such as peas, beans, soy, and peanuts.
Synonym or Restatement	A word that means the same as the unfamiliar word	The **epidermis**, or skin, is the largest organ of the human body.
Antonym or Contrast	A word that means the opposite of the unfamiliar word	A person who commits **treason** is not loyal to his country.
Cause and Effect	What happens and why	I was **exuberant** when summer vacation started.

Try It

Read the passage. As you read, circle unfamiliar words. Underline context clues that help you understand each word's meaning. Use the questions to help you.

adapted from

The Time Machine
by H.G. Wells

I shared a cab with the Editor. He thought the tale a "gaudy lie." For my own part I was unable to come to a conclusion. The story was so fantastic and incredible, the telling so credible and sober. I lay awake most of the night thinking about it. I determined to go the next day and see the Time Traveler again. I was told he was in the laboratory, and being on easy terms in the house, I went up to him. The laboratory, however, was empty. I stared for a minute at the Time Machine and put out my hand and touched the lever. At that the squat substantial-looking mass swayed like a bough shaken by the wind. Its instability startled me extremely, and I had a queer reminiscence of the childish days when I used to be forbidden to meddle. I came back through the corridor. The Time Traveler met me in the smoking-room. He was coming from the house. He had a small camera under one arm and a knapsack under the other. He laughed when he saw me, and gave me an elbow to shake. "I'm frightfully busy," said he, "with that thing in there."

> What does *instability* mean? Where do you find words that tell you about it?

> What is a *reminiscence*? What words give you clues?

"But is it not some hoax?" I said. "Do you really travel through time?"

"Really and truly I do." And he looked frankly into my eyes. He hesitated. His eye wandered about the room. "I only want half an hour," he said. "I know why you came, and it's awfully good of you. There are some magazines here. If you'll stop to lunch I'll prove you this time traveling up to the hilt, specimen and all. If you'll forgive my leaving you now?"

I consented, hardly comprehending then the full import of his words, and he nodded and went on down the corridor. I heard the door of the laboratory slam, seated myself in a chair, and took up a daily paper. What was he going to do before lunchtime? Then suddenly I was reminded by an advertisement that I had promised to meet Richardson, the publisher, at two. I looked at my watch, and saw that I could barely save that engagement. I got up and went down the passage to tell the Time Traveler.

Continued on the next page ➡

Continued from the previous page

As I took hold of the handle of the door I heard an exclamation, oddly truncated at the end, and a click and a thud. A gust of air whirled round me as I opened the door, and from within came the sound of broken glass falling on the floor. The Time Traveler was not there. I seemed to see a ghostly, indistinct figure sitting in a whirling mass of black and brass for a moment—a figure so transparent that the bench behind with its sheets of drawings was absolutely distinct; but this phantasm vanished as I rubbed my eyes.

The Time Machine had gone. Save for a subsiding stir of dust, the further end of the laboratory was empty. A pane of the skylight had, apparently, just been blown in.

I felt an unreasonable amazement. I knew that something strange had happened, and for the moment could not distinguish what the strange thing might be. As I stood staring, the door into the garden opened, and the man-servant appeared.

Based on this passage, what does *transparent* mean?

How can you figure out the meaning of *phantasm*?

What should you do if you cannot find context clues near an unfamiliar word?

Apply It

Read the passage. Answer the questions that follow.

Jackie Robinson—Breaking the Color Line

It is important to remember those who fought to overcome social impediments. We must not forget people such as Jackie Robinson, who became the first African American to play Major League Baseball since it had become segregated in 1889. Before Robinson broke the color line, great African American baseball players had to play in a separate league, known as the Negro Baseball League. Legendary players like Satchel Paige wowed crowds with their talent. Nonetheless, the Negro League players were paid poorly compared to their Major League counterparts. Yet for a long time, desegregation of the sport seemed impossible.

Jack Roosevelt Robinson, born in Cairo, Georgia, in 1919, was outstanding at sports. In high school, he won the Junior Boys' Singles Championship at the Pacific Coast Negro Tennis Tournament. After high school, Robinson went to UCLA, where he excelled at baseball, basketball, football, and track. But it was his proficiency at baseball that attracted the attention of Branch Rickey, the owner of the Brooklyn Dodgers.

After seeing Robinson play shortstop on the Negro League's Kansas City Monarchs, Rickey invited Robinson to play baseball for a Dodgers farm team called the Montreal Royals in 1945. Because Robinson won acclaim for fielding and batting, Rickey asked Robinson to join the Dodgers in 1947. Rickey warned Robinson that as the first black Major Leaguer, he would hear attacks and insults. The Dodgers' owner asked Robinson to accept these in silence. Rickey believed that was the only way that a wide fan base would come to accept integrated teams. Robinson agreed.

At the end of that first season, Robinson won Rookie of the Year. Just two years later, he was named Most Valuable Player. In 1955, he contributed to the Dodgers successful effort to win the World Series. Having played a decade of Major League Baseball, in 1957 Robinson announced that he was retiring. After retiring, he was a vice-president for the coffee company, Chock Full O' Nuts, from 1957 until 1964. He also worked for the NAACP (the National Association for the Advancement of Colored People), raising funds and giving speeches on the organization's behalf.

Continued on the next page ▶

Continued from the previous page

During his Major League Baseball career, Robinson showed tremendous courage and discipline. Although Robinson encountered countless instances of racism from people in the stands and even from some of his own teammates, he focused on playing ball. Many fervent fans supported him, and he became one of the best and most popular baseball players. He was inducted into the Baseball Hall of Fame in 1962—the first African American to receive this honor. Robinson received another accolade on the fiftieth anniversary of his historic desegregation of baseball, when his uniform number, 42, was retired from professional baseball.

Robinson was a hero throughout the African American community. In fact, as an educated man who didn't drink, smoke, or lose his temper in public, he was an excellent role model for young people of all races. Though he died after a heart attack in 1972, Robinson's achievements on and off the field live on.

Use "Jackie Robinson" to answer the questions. Write your answers in complete sentences.

1. What does the word *impediments* most likely mean?

_____

_____

2. What words help you figure out the meaning of *impediments*?

_____

_____

3. What does the word *excelled* mean?

_____

_____

4. What is another word you could use for *acclaim*?

_____

_____

5. As used in the passage, what does the word *fervent* mean?

_____

_____

6. What context clues help you figure out the meaning of *accolade*?

_____

_____

Roots and Affixes

Learn About It

A **root** is the basic word to which other word parts can be added. A root gives a word its main meaning. An **affix** is a word part that is added before or after a root. A **prefix** is an affix added at the beginning of a root word. For example, *un-* means "not," and *trans-* means "across." A **suffix** is an affix added at the end of a root word. For example, *-less* means "without," and *-ly* means "in a way." The suffix *-ology* means "the study of." When you understand how affixes change the meaning of a root word, you can figure out what the new word means.

Read the paragraph. Look for roots, prefixes, and suffixes.

For many years, transoceanic telephone calls were impossible. Then, a telephone line was laid under the ocean. For the first time, a citizen in the United States could quickly speak with people in different countries of Europe.

Root	Meaning	Example
Arch	First, chief	Matriarchy, architect
Civ	Citizen	Civilization, civics
Chron	Time	Chronology, chronic
Dent	Tooth	Dentist, denture
Prin, prim	First	Principle, primary
Terr	Earth	Territory, terrestrial

Try It

Read the passage. Underline words that have prefixes or suffixes. Use the questions to help you.

Dental Discoveries

Dentistry has been around for thousands of years. Looking at the chronology of dental discoveries shows that somewhat sophisticated practices in tooth care had no basis in science. For example, according to archaeological findings in Pakistan, people had their teeth drilled as far back as 9000–7500 BCE. Archaeologists are not sure whether the molars that they found were drilled to relieve pain or to change the person's appearance. The people might have had their teeth drilled to get rid of evil spirits.

> **What root do *chronology* and *chronicled* share?**

People living in ancient civilizations probably did not have quite as much tooth decay as individuals have today. In those times, sugar was not as plentiful, and there were no highly processed foods. However, because people had to chew unprocessed food thoroughly, their teeth did get worn down.

Ancient writing shows that Sumerians around 5000 BCE believed a toothworm caused tooth decay. Apparently, this belief was widespread. In fact, the German abbess Hildegard was still writing about how to get rid of the toothworm in the 12th century. She believed that the person suffering from tooth decay should burn aloe and wood and hold their head above the fire.

The first chronicled mention of a toothache is found in ancient Egyptian medical texts from around 3500 BCE. Another record shows that gum swelling was treated there with a concoction of cumin, other spices, and onion around 3000 BCE.

> ***Archaeological* is a form of the word *archaeology*. What does the word *archaeology* mean? Look at the meanings of the word parts *arch* and *logy*.**

Primitive treatments for toothaches were used in China as early as 2700 BCE. The Greeks wrote about using wires as part of dental treatment during the years 500–300 BCE. Today, it is common for people to wear braces. By the 7th century, the Chinese and Romans filled cavities with a fusion of metals in the same way materials are combined to make fillings today. Romans also used dentures that were made from various materials, including bone or wood.

Dental hygiene was also practiced throughout the ancient world. Ancient Romans used gold picks to clean their teeth after their lengthy dinner parties. In 3rd century Greece, citizens habitually cleaned their teeth by using crushed mint to remove food particles.

Continued on the next page ➤

Continued from the previous page

Many ancient practices seem positively bizarre to us today. The Roman writer Pliny the Elder suggested that if an individual had a toothache, he or she should find a frog by light of a full moon and request that it relieve the pain. Ancient Egyptians believed if someone had a toothache, he or she should place a recently deceased mouse near the aching tooth, in order to relieve pain.

> **What root do** *dental* **and** *dentistry* **share?**

Not all dental practices were focused on relieving pain or preventing decay. In Central America, the ancient Maya sometimes drilled small holes in their teeth and decorated their teeth with jade or other minerals. They also filed and sharpened their teeth. Archaeologists have found evidence that the Maya used shells to replace missing teeth.

While some of these practices may seem senseless today, it is clear that ancient civilizations practiced rudimentary dentistry. Those who first made extractions, fillings, and dentures paved the way for the dentists of our time.

> **What does the word** *senseless* **mean? Think about the meaning of the suffix** *-less*.

HOTS Understand

Explain how knowing the meaning of common affixes can help you figure out the meanings of new words.

Apply It

Read the passage. Answer the questions that follow.

The Vast Inca Empire

The largest civilization in pre-Columbian America belonged to the Inca. With its principle city in Cusco, a city in what is now Peru, their empire covered Peru, Bolivia, and parts of Ecuador and Chile. The empire reached into present-day Argentina in the south and Colombia in the north. Scholars believe that the Inca state began between 1200 and 1300 CE.

Despite the fact that the Inca had such a vast empire, archaeologists have not had as much evidence to study as they would have hoped for. Unlike the Maya, the Inca did not have a written language. Also, when the Spanish explorers came to America, they were impressed by the wealthy civilization. Receiving permission from their queen to conquer the Inca, the Spanish then destroyed the palaces of the Inca's capital and built their own on the ruins.

Nonetheless, some great architecture from the Incan Empire remains, including the famed town of Machu Picchu. Incan builders expertly sculpted massive rocks so that they fit together perfectly, and this made their buildings able to withstand the centuries.

Recently, archaeologists have found numerous sites where they have discovered more about the Inca. The early Inca had fertile soil and a source of water at Cusco, which was especially important in the 12th century, when a severe drought overtook much of the surrounding land. By the 13th century, the Inca at Cusco were using terraced farming methods and could grow more food than they needed. Because they had an abundance of food, people were able to spend time doing things other than farming and hunting. Armies could now be formed, and Inca rulers were interested in conquest. When possible, the Inca used diplomacy to gain power over their neighbors. When diplomacy failed, they fought. In the 15th century, the Inca battled the Colla people who lived south of Cusco. Since the Colla had a wealth of resources, it was especially important to the Inca rulers that the Inca army should defeat them. When the Inca conquered the Colla, they built roads in their new territory and organized civic life.

Continued on the next page ➤

Continued from the previous page

The Inca used irrigation and sophisticated farming methods very successfully. They created storehouses for surplus food, and kept track of exactly how much of each crop they had. At the height of their empire, the Inca controlled most of western South America. Each region of the empire had to give provisions to the ruling powers. They also had to store provisions for Inca troops to use.

Inca rulers were active in matters of religious and civic life as well as warfare. They also built magnificent country retreats where they entertained. When the kings died, their bodies were mummified. Even the deceased kings were held in awe and treated respectfully. When the Spaniards first tried to conquer the Inca, they captured their king, Atahualpa. After eight months, they killed the revered ruler. The Spanish chose a teenager from the royal family to take over as king. Soon this teenager, Manco Inca, grew angry with the invaders and tried to defeat them at Cusco. Though he didn't succeed, Manco Inca was able to escape. He continued to mount attacks against the Spanish from a remote city in the jungle. Túpac Amaru was the last indigenous leader of the Inca. The Spanish slaughtered Túpac and his remaining army in 1572, which marked the tragic demise of a great empire.

Use "The Vast Inca Empire" to answer the questions. Write your answers in complete sentences.

1. What root do the words *civilization* and *civic* share? What do the words mean?

_____

_____

2. What does the word *principle* mean?

_____

_____

3. What root do the words *archaeologists* and *architecture* share? What do the words mean?

_____

_____

4. What root do the words *terraced* and *territory* share? What does each word mean?

_____

_____

5. What does the word *respectfully* mean? How do the root and affix combine in this word?

_____

_____

Use Reference Materials

Learn About It

A **dictionary** is a book that lists words in alphabetical order. It includes definitions for each word, along with a pronunciation guide. If one word has multiple meanings, the dictionary will include definitions for each meaning. A **glossary** is a list of important words found at the back of some books. A glossary will include the meaning of a word as it relates to its use in the book. A **thesaurus** gives a list of synonyms and sometimes antonyms for each entry.

Read the glossary entry, the dictionary entry, and the thesaurus entry below. Then review the chart that follows.

Glossary Entry:
trench a long narrow ditch with steep sides used by soldiers for protection in battle

Dictionary Entry:
trench (trench) *noun* **1.** a ditch with soil piled on the sides **2.** a depression in the ocean floor *verb* **3.** to dig a trench

Thesaurus Entry:
trench
Synonyms: dike, gutter, trough

Glossary	Dictionary	Thesaurus
Gives the meaning of the word for the book in which it is found	Gives more than one meaning	Gives synonyms for the word
Includes a definition	Includes a definition	Sometimes lists antonyms for the words
Sometimes includes a pronunciation guide	Includes a pronunciation guide	
	Gives the word's parts of speech	
	Shows the word's syllables	

Try It

Read the passage. As you read, pay attention to the meaning of the highlighted words. Think about whether the words have more than one meaning. Circle other words that have more than one meaning. Use the questions to help you.

A Sheep Named Dolly

When scientists in Scotland first announced that they had successfully cloned a sheep, people all over the world took notice. The clone, named Dolly, was the first animal to be cloned from an adult animal's cells. The experiment led to a debate about whether such a procedure was ethical or for the best.

> What does the word *cloned* mean in the first sentence of the passage?

Those against cloning believed that the whole procedure was unnatural, because it required such extreme scientific intervention. They also worried that animals that resulted from the process could be unhealthy, and that they might cause problems that science could not predict.

> What does the word *clone* mean in the second sentence?

Those in favor of animal cloning believed that science would benefit and that the benefits would outweigh the costs to society. The process by which Dolly was cloned could also lead to scientists being able to genetically modify cells to produce desired results. This could lead to important advances in medicine. Additionally, they believed that scientists could successfully manage cloning animals so that the clones would not be sickly or abnormal.

> What does the word *debate* mean in the first paragraph of the passage?

All of this occurred in the 1990s. How did Dolly's life have an impact on the debate?

On the one hand, Dolly lived like most other sheep that are kept indoors, although she was studied more than others. The famous clone was able to mate and reproduce. Dolly was mother to six lambs in all.

Continued on the next page ➤

Continued from the previous page

On the other hand, Dolly did develop arthritis at a fairly early age. This led to speculation that clones produced from adult cells aged prematurely. Scientists still debate the cause of the early arthritis. Dolly was euthanized at a fairly early age—at about six and a half years, when sheep often lived up to twelve years. However, she was suffering from a disease that any indoor sheep could contract, a contagious virus.

Since Dolly came to fame, there have been many other examples of animals being cloned, though it is still a very expensive and tricky procedure. Rather oddly, some people use cloning to try to duplicate their experience with a beloved animal. When the original animal is ill, these people use biotechnology firms to create the animal's genetic duplicate. Horse owners have even used cloning to create duplicates of racing champions. Of course, these new animals are not exactly the same as the animals they replace, any more than an identical human twin is exactly the same as his or her twin. For now, horse racing forbids clones from entering competitions.

What does the word *debate* mean in the sixth paragraph?

What are two meanings for the word *duplicate*, as the word is used in the last paragraph?

Apply It

Read the passage. Answer the questions that follow.

The Swim Meet

As Sherri warmed up for the 100-meter freestyle race, she felt confident and quick. She had been working on her stroke, and her arm movements felt strong and effortless. Sherri had a distinguished record as a swimmer; locally, she was undefeated for her age group. Now she was swimming at the district championship, and she knew she would compete against other excellent athletes.

But when Sherri actually saw the other swimmers she would be competing against in the race, she realized that she might not maintain her winning streak. She became nervous to an unprecedented degree. The girls were all sleek and muscular, and they moved with precision and grace.

Sherri was tempted to decline to be in the race. She had had a vision of being a championship swimmer for as long as she could remember, but up until now, winning had come easily. Yes, she worked hard, but she loved the sport. With her natural ability and hard work, she had distinguished herself from the competition. For the first time, she realized that at some point, her days of winning would decline.

As Sherri watched the other girls head to the race's starting point, she found that she was too nervous to move. Just then Sherri's coach, Ms. Hitchcock, came into view.

"Sherri," she shouted. "What are you doing? Come on, the race is about to start!" Hearing her coach's voice, Sherri sprang into action. With a stroke of luck, Sherri knew that she might win again.

Continued on the next page ▶

Continued from the previous page

When she dove into the pool, the temperature of the water was exactly 78.5 degrees Fahrenheit. As she stroked the water, she felt the weeks and months of training taking hold. Yes, she knew that one day she would begin to lose races. Nonetheless, she was determined that she would win today.

Dictionary Entry:
stroke (strohk) *verb* **1.** to move the arm and hand when swimming *noun* **2.** a movement of the arms for swimming **3.** a sudden instance or occurrence **4.** a serious disruption to blood flow in the brain

Dictionary Entry:
distinguished (di STING wisht) *adjective* **1.** recognized as excellent *verb* **2.** to have performed well and received recognition

Dictionary Entry:
decline (DEE kline) *verb* **1.** to slope downwards **2.** to show unwillingness in accepting or participating in *noun* **3.** a slow sinking or wasting away of **4.** a downward slope

Use "The Swim Meet" to answer the questions. Use a dictionary to look up unfamiliar words. Write your answers in complete sentences.

1. What does *stroke* mean in the sentence "With a stroke of luck, Sherri knew that she might win again"?

_____

_____

2. What does *stroke* mean in the sentence, "As she stroked the water, she felt the weeks and months of training taking hold"?

_____

_____

3. What is another definition for the word *stroke*?

_____

_____

4. What does *distinguished* mean in the sentence "Sherri had a distinguished record"?

_____

_____

5. What does *distinguished* mean in the sentence "she had distinguished herself from the competition"?

_____

_____

6. What part of speech is the word *decline* in the sentence, "Sherri was tempted to decline to be in the race"?

_____

_____

Figures of Speech

Learn About It

Figurative language is phrases or expressions used to make speech and writing more interesting. **Figures of speech** are one type of figurative language. Some figures of speech **allude**, or make reference to, mythology, history, or classic works.

Read the sentences. Look for a figure of speech and think about what it means. Then review the chart below.

"Coach," Diego called. "I'm worried that my brother will meet his Waterloo today."

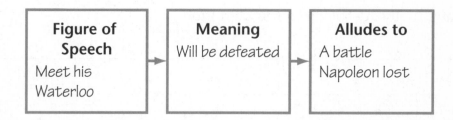

| **Figure of Speech** | → | **Meaning** | → | **Alludes to** |
| Meet his Waterloo | | Will be defeated | | A battle Napoleon lost |

Some Figures of Speech		
Allusion	**Source**	**Explanation**
Achilles's heel	Mythology	Achilles's only weak spot was his heel.
Albatross	"The Rime of the Ancient Mariner" by Samuel Taylor Coleridge	An albatross follows the mariner's ship during stormy weather. The crew thinks it is a symbol of luck. The mariner kills the albatross, which the crew hangs around the mariner's neck.
Helen of Troy	Mythology	Helen's beauty started the Trojan War and caused a thousand ships to be launched.
Hercules	Mythology	Hercules was very strong.
Midas touch	Mythology	King Midas could turn anything he touched into gold.

Try It

Read the passage. Look at the phrases that are highlighted. Use the questions to help you.

adapted from

Frankenstein, or the Modern Prometheus
by Mary Wollstonecraft (Godwin) Shelley

To Mrs. Saville, England Archangel, 28th March, 17—

How slowly the time passes here, encompassed as I am by frost and snow! Yet a second step is taken towards my enterprise. I have hired a vessel and am occupied in collecting my sailors; those whom I have already engaged appear to be men on whom I can depend and are certainly possessed of dauntless courage.

But I have one want which I have never yet been able to satisfy, and the absence of the object of which I now feel as a most severe evil. I have no friend, Margaret: when I am glowing with the enthusiasm of success, there will be none to participate my joy; if I am assailed by disappointment, no one will endeavor to sustain me in dejection. I shall commit my thoughts to paper, it is true; but that is a poor medium for the communication of feeling. I desire the company of a man who could sympathize with me, whose eyes would reply to mine. Yet do not suppose, because I complain a little or because I can conceive a consolation for my toils which I may never know, that I am wavering in my resolutions. Those are as fixed as fate, and my voyage is only now delayed until the weather shall permit my setting off. The winter has been dreadfully severe, but the spring promises well, and it is considered as a remarkably early season, so that perhaps I may sail sooner than I expected. I shall do nothing rashly: you know me sufficiently to confide in my prudence and considerateness whenever the safety of others is committed to my care.

> In Greek mythology, Prometheus is a Titan who steals fire from Zeus and gives it to human beings. Zeus does not want mortals to have this power, and punishes Prometheus severely.

> In the book *Frankenstein*, the title refers to the scientist who brings a monster made from parts of corpses to life. Why do you think Shelley refers to him as a "modern Prometheus"?

Continued on the next page ➤

Continued from the previous page

I cannot describe to you my sensations on the near prospect of my undertaking. It is impossible to communicate to you trembling sensation, half pleasurable and half fearful, with which I am preparing to depart. I am going to unexplored regions, to "the land of mist and snow," but I shall kill no albatross; therefore do not be alarmed for my safety or if I should come back to you as worn and woeful as the "Ancient Mariner." You will smile at my allusion, but I will disclose a secret. I have often attributed my attachment to, my passionate enthusiasm for, the dangerous mysteries of ocean to that production of the most imaginative of modern poets. There is something at work in my soul which I do not understand. I am practically industrious—painstaking, a workman to execute with perseverance and labor—but besides this there is a love for the marvelous, a belief in the marvelous, intertwined in all my projects, which hurries me out of the common pathways of men, even to the wild sea and unvisited regions I am about to explore. But to return to dearer considerations. Shall I meet you again, after having traversed immense seas, and returned by the most southern cape of Africa or America? I dare not expect such success, yet I cannot bear to look on the reverse of the picture. Continue for the present to write to me at every opportunity: I may receive your letters on some occasions when I need them most to support my spirits. I love you very tenderly. Remember me with affection, should you never hear from me again.

Your affectionate brother,

Robert Walton

The highlighted phrases allude to the poem "The Rime of the Ancient Mariner" by Samuel Taylor Coleridge.

The second highlighted phrase refers to the fact that the mariner sorely regrets killing the albatross.

Why do authors include allusions in their works?

Apply It

Read the passage. Then answer the questions on the next page.

Allusive Ads

One afternoon, Maria was sitting on the porch, leafing through a glossy magazine. Before long, she looked at an ad and snorted.

"Listen to this," she said to her sixteen-year-old brother Pablo. "'Would you like to have a face that could launch a thousand ships? Try *Miraculous* Skin Cream. The results are legendary!' Ha! I'm sure if I buy it, I'll look like Helen of Troy in no time."

"Maybe you should try it," laughed Pablo.

"Yeah, right! I want to be just like this woman in the ad, staring narcissistically at her own reflection. I'll buy this cream as soon as you buy this weight-lifting program. Check out the ad. 'Have the strength of Hercules in forty days or less.'"

"Huh, I guess advertisers think that being afraid to be called a weakling is every boy's Achilles's heel. Luckily, I know these ads are bogus. I don't even think that's the same guy in the 'After' picture!"

"I know, right?" said Maria. "Oh, here's one for Mom and Dad. 'You, too, can sell our amazing product from the comfort of your home. You may find you have the Midas touch.'"

"It'd be nice to have a little more gold around here, but I think they missed the point of that story," said Pablo. "King Midas turns his own daughter into gold. Hey, wait a minute, maybe this isn't such a bad idea!"

"Ha, ha," Maria said sarcastically. "You're a regular court jester. But seriously, how can anyone believe these ads?"

"Well, they're not all lies. Besides, people like to hope that things can change," said Pablo.

"I guess," said Maria. "But do you really think you'll be some big Adonis if you dress the way they do in these ads?"

"Well, look at this ad for a jacket," Pablo said. "You've got to admit I would look pretty sharp in that."

"Are you thinking about your big date next weekend?" Maria laughed. "You're quite the Romeo with your new girlfriend."

Continued on the next page ➤

Continued from the previous page

"Yeah, well, my date isn't going to end in tragedy like Shakespeare's play," Pablo said.

"Well, while you're off with your busy social life, I think I'm going to write these advertisers and complain about how they're misleading people," said Maria.

"That's pointless," said Pablo. "Advertisers have been doing this for a long time. The Romans had an expression they used: *Caveat emptor.* That translates into 'buyer beware.'"

"I don't see any harm in letting them know what I think," said Maria. "Maybe some advertisers or the business people behind these products would listen to me. I'll just explain that I'd be more likely to buy their product if they didn't exaggerate so much."

"Advertisers mostly want to get your attention," said Pablo. "That way, buyers are more apt to remember the name of their product. From the way you're acting, it looks like they did their job."

"They got my attention all right," said Maria. "Now I'm going to try to get theirs!"

Use "Allusive Ads" to answer the questions. Write your answers in complete sentences.

1. Based on what you know and the context in the story, what does "a face that could launch a thousand ships" allude to?

_____

_____

2. Why would buyers want a product that would give them "the strength of Hercules"?

_____

_____

3. What does Pablo mean when he talks about advertisers thinking that being thought of as a weakling is every boy's "Achilles's heel"?

_____

_____

4. What does "the Midas touch" mean? What story is it alluding to?

_____

_____

5. What does Maria mean by saying, "You're quite the Romeo"?

_____

_____

Analogies

Learn About It

An **analogy** is the relationship between two words or concepts. Usually, in an analogy, one thing is compared to another. When you are trying to determine a word's meaning, you can look at how that word is related to another word. Analogies are sometimes written as *liquid : solid :: bright : dim*. That would read: *"Liquid is to solid as bright is to dim."*

Read the paragraph. Look for analogies. Then look at examples of analogies in the chart bellow.

A smart phone is like an old fashioned phone in the same way that a computer is like an old-fashioned adding machine. They have things in common, but the smart phone and the computer can do far more than their predecessors.

Analogies		
Types of Analogies	**First Analogy**	**Second Analogy**
One Thing Is Like Another	Fast: quick ::	Tiny : small
	Loud: noisy ::	Rough : coarse
One Thing is the Opposite of Another	Dark: light ::	Day : night
	Fancy: simple ::	Short: tall
One Thing Is a Part of Another	Toe: foot ::	Finger: hand
	Chapter: book ::	Scene : movie

Try It

Read the poems. Think about the relationship between the highlighted words.
Use the questions to help you.

The Day Is Done
by Henry Wadsworth Longfellow

The day is done, and the darkness
Falls from the wings of Night,
As a feather is wafted downward
From an eagle in his flight.

5   I see the lights of the village
Gleam through the rain and the mist,
And a feeling of sadness comes o'er me
That my soul cannot resist:

A feeling of sadness and longing,
10   That is not akin to pain,
And resembles sorrow only
As the mist resembles the rain.

> What is the relationship between *mist* and *rain*? What does that tell you about the narrator's sadness?

Come, read to me some poem,
Some simple and heartfelt lay,
15   That shall soothe this restless feeling,
And banish the thoughts of day.

Not from the grand old masters,
Not from the bards sublime,
Whose distant footsteps echo
20   Through the corridors of Time.

> What is the relationship between the words *grand* and *humbler*? What is the relationship between the words *toil* and *rest*?

For, like strains of martial music,
Their mighty thoughts suggest
Life's endless toil and endeavor;
And tonight I long for rest.

25   Read from some humbler poet,
Whose songs gushed from his heart,
As showers from the clouds of summer,
Or tears from the eyelids start.

Loss and Gain

by Henry Wadsworth Longfellow

When I compare
What I have lost with what I have gained,
What I have missed with what attained,
Little room do I find for pride.

5   I am aware
How many days have been idly spent;
How like an arrow the good intent
Has fallen short or been turned aside.

But who shall dare
10   To measure loss and gain in this wise?
Defeat may be victory in disguise;
The lowest ebb is the turn of the tide.

> *Lost* and *gained* are antonyms. If *missed* and *attained* are also antonyms, what does *attained* mean?

> What is the relationship between the words *victory* and *defeat*?

HOTS Understand

Explain how analogies can convey an idea or a mental image in ways that straight-forward prose cannot.

Apply It

Read the passage. Answer the questions on the next page.

excerpted from "The Minotaur"

Tanglewood Tales

by Nathaniel Hawthorne

When Theseus was ushered into the royal apartment, the only object that he seemed to behold was the white-bearded old king. There he sat on his magnificent throne, a dazzling crown on his head, and a scepter in his hand. His aspect was stately and majestic, although his years and infirmities weighed heavily upon him, as if each year were a lump of lead, and each infirmity a ponderous stone, and all were bundled up together, and laid upon his weary shoulders. The tears both of joy and sorrow sprang into the young man's eyes; for he thought how sad it was to see his dear father so infirm, and how sweet it would be to support him with his own youthful strength, and to cheer him up with the alacrity of his loving spirit. When a son takes a father into his warm heart, it renews the old man's youth in a better way than by the heat of Medea's magic caldron. And this was what Theseus resolved to do. He could scarcely wait to see whether King Aegeus would recognize him, so eager was he to throw himself into his arms.

Advancing to the foot of the throne, he attempted to make a little speech, which he had been thinking about, as he came up the stairs. But he was almost choked by a great many tender feelings that gushed out of his heart and swelled into his throat, all struggling to find utterance together. And therefore, unless he could have laid his full, over-brimming heart into the king's hand, poor Theseus knew not what to do or say. The cunning Medea observed what was passing in the young man's mind. She was more wicked at that moment than ever she had been before; for (and it makes me tremble to tell you of it) she did her worst to turn all this unspeakable love with which Theseus was agitated to his own ruin and destruction.

"Does your majesty see his confusion?" she whispered in the king's ear.

"He is so conscious of guilt, that he trembles and cannot speak. The wretch lives too long! Quick! Offer him the wine!"

Continued on the next page ▶

Continued from the previous page

Now King Aegeus had been gazing earnestly at the young stranger, as he drew near the throne. There was something, he knew not what, either in his white brow, or in the fine expression of his mouth, or in his beautiful and tender eyes, that made him indistinctly feel as if he had seen this youth before; as if, indeed, he had trotted him on his knee when a baby, and had beheld him growing to be a stalwart man, while he himself grew old. But Medea guessed how the king felt, and would not suffer him to yield to these natural sensibilities; although they were the voice of his deepest heart, telling him as plainly as it could speak, that here was our dear son, and Aethra's son, coming to claim him for a father. The enchantress again whispered in the king's ear, and compelled him, by her witchcraft, to see everything under a false aspect.

Use "Tanglewood Tales" to answer the questions. Write your answers in complete sentences.

 1. *Magnificent* and *dazzling* are synonyms. If *stately* and *majestic* are also synonyms, what does the word *stately* mean?

_____

_____

 2. What is being compared to *lead* and *stone* in the first paragraph?

_____

_____

 3. If *joy* is to *sorrow* as *strength* is to *infirmity*, what does *infirmity* mean?

_____

_____

4. If *joy* is to *cheer* as *alacrity* is to *eager*, what does *alacrity* mean?

_____

_____

 5. *Gushed* and *over-brimming* describe Theseus's feelings. With what are they being compared?

_____

_____

 6. How is the word *seen* related to the word *beheld*?

_____

_____

Denotation and Connotation

Learn About It

A word can have two different kinds of meaning. **Denotation** is a word's literal, dictionary meaning. **Connotation** is a word's emotional meaning.

Read the paragraph. Think of the different connotations of the highlighted words. Then look at more examples of denotation and connotation in the chart below.

Did you enjoy the new musical theater production? I thought that the set was garish, but I did enjoy the dazzling costumes. It was fun to see our friends singing and dancing under that bright light.

Some Words and Their Denotations and Connotations			
Word	**Denotation**	**Connotation**	**Example**
Aroma	Smell, odor, scent	Enticing smell, usually emanating from food	The **aroma** of the baking chicken brought me to the kitchen.
Fragrance	Smell, odor, scent	Pleasing smell, as from perfume	The perfume had a sweet **fragrance**.
Stench	Smell, odor, scent	Unpleasant and revolting smell, as in sewage	The **stench** of sulfur in the lab was overwhelming.

Try It

Read the passage. Think about the connotations of the highlighted words. Use the questions to help you.

The New Teacher

"I've heard our new social studies teacher tells really great stories during class," said Harry.

"Where'd you hear that?" asked Daelani.

"My cousin," Harry said. "She used to teach eighth grade at his school. My cousin said that he learned more from Ms. Crabtree than from any other teacher."

> Would you rather listen to a *story* or a *lecture*? How does each word make you feel?

"Ms. Crabtree, huh? Is she one of those teachers who gives really long lectures without letting anyone else talk?" asked Daelani.

"What are you two talking about?" said Chris, as he approached them.

"Harry says our new teacher tells stories, and that's all good, but I hope she doesn't just drone on and on," Daelani said.

> Would you rather listen to someone *talk* or *drone*?

"I didn't say she gave monologues," laughed Harry. "My cousin told me that she tells amazing stories about how things used to be. I'm sure she'll let you get a word in."

"I'm just afraid that your idea of an amazing story is my idea of a boring lecture," grumbled Daelani.

"Way to start the year with a positive attitude," laughed Chris.

"Oh, stop now," said Daelani. "Social studies is my favorite subject. I just like classes where there's lots of discussion. Is that so wrong?"

"Well, it wouldn't be, except that some people just prattle on and on. It seems like they have to say every thought that comes into their heads," Chris said.

> What word can you replace *say* with that has a similar connotation to *prattle*?

"Well, I like hearing what everyone has to say," Daelani countered. "Besides, if it's just the teacher talking, I might fall right to sleep."

Continued on the next page ➤

Continued from the previous page

Just then the bell rang, so they walked toward their classroom together. As they entered, they saw a tall, handsome woman standing in the back of the class. She wore a flaming red scarf and a burgundy sweater, so she was hard to miss. Daelani, Chris, and Harry saw that the chairs were arranged in a circle, so that everyone could see one another. Many of their classmates were already seated, looking a little nervous about taking part in the new class. Soon all the chairs were filled with students. They turned to the woman at the back of the class, who looked calmly back at them. While the students looked apprehensive, their teacher looked confident and at ease.

> **Would you rather be *nervous* or *apprehensive*?**

"Good morning, class," she said warmly. "I'm Ms. Crabtree, and as you may know, I'm just starting at your school. What do you think I should know?"

Daelani's hand shot up, and she spoke before anyone else. "My name's Daelani," she chirped. "Welcome to the school, Ms. Crabtree. I've been going here since last year, so I can help you out."

Chris and Harry smiled at each other. It looked like Daelani's worries were over.

HOTS Analyze

Why should writers pay particular attention to the connotations of words they use?

Apply It

Read the passage. Answer the questions on the next page.

Robots That Care

How should we care for our elderly? Many seniors would like to live at home for as long as possible, but, with families living in different cities, who can help them stay independent? Some companies are suggesting an interesting possibility—robots.

The robots being developed are equipped with body sensors. These will allow them to find the person they are attending to and to provide them with valuable options for communicating with the outside world. One company is making a robot that looks humanoid and holds a computer screen in an easel. Other companies are making robots that do not attempt to look human. So far, most of the models use computer screens, so that a person can communicate through Skype™ and social networking programs. They also have basic speech recognition so that the elderly will be able to give the robots voice commands. Multiple artificial intelligence programs will allow the robot to keep track of schedules and medical appointments. Companies are exploring possibilities for the robots to track individuals' blood pressure and heart rate. The robots could then communicate a patients' conditions to their doctor or family members. One wheelchair robot is in development that could perform vital tasks for its owners, including getting them from place to place, helping them communicate with others at a distance, and tracking their health.

In Japan, the robots are already at work. One named Paro has been placed with patients in nursing care facilities who are suffering from dementia. Paro is made to look like a cute baby seal, and responds to its name. Apparently, even patients who had stopped communicating with friends and family have responded to the adorable robot. The nursing home patients hold and cuddle the robot, seeming to enjoy the act of giving care (even if it is illusory).

As robotic care enters the marketplace, some medical ethicists worry about what the use of robots means for our future. Are we giving up some of our humanity by offloading our care-giving work to robots? Proponents of the technology say that supplementing human care-givers with robots will make everyone happier in the process. Enemies look at the fact that, so far, robots are marketed to do tasks for the less capable members of society. Does this mean we see these people as less valuable?

Continued on the next page ➤

Continued from the previous page

Yet robots are also being developed to serve people in the prime of life. One has been developed as a diet coach. It asks you about your progress every day, and responds with helpful encouragement. It's possible to imagine robots eventually helping people with all sorts of goals, from quitting smoking to learning a new language to exercising more.

There are fascinating psychological questions about how these robots can become a person's companion, even a sort of friend. Even people who do not have dementia seem to enjoy their visits with Paro, fully aware that it is a robot. Perhaps the robots being developed to help the elderly stay at home longer will have a similarly reassuring, responsive presence. People living alone, especially, could come to rely on and feel affection for such a robot. Is there anything wrong with loving a machine?

Use "Robots That Care" to answer the questions. Write your answers in complete sentences.

1. What does *elderly* mean? What does it connote?

_____

_____

2. What word could you use instead of *interesting* to connote a greater degree of optimism?

_____

_____

3. Which word has a stronger connotation, *valuable* or *vital*?

_____

_____

4. What does *cuddle* connote?

_____

_____

5. What is the difference between *offloading* and *supplementing*?

_____

_____

6. Which word should you use instead of *enemies* to avoid a confrontational connotation?

_____

_____

Academic Vocabulary

Learn About It

Academic vocabulary is made up of the words that are useful to know for particular subject areas, such as math, science, and social studies. If you do not know the meaning of a word, you can look it up in a glossary or dictionary.

Read the paragraph. Use the charts below to identify academic vocabulary words.

In some developing countries, many people depend on subsistence farming as a vital source of nutrition. People sometimes struggle to find enough potable water in the rural areas. The infrastructure for water delivery is not in place.

Science Vocabulary	Meaning
Microorganism	A microscopic living thing
Nutrition	The process of being nourished
Fungus	An organism that produces spores
Natural resource	Things found in nature that are useful to human beings
Potable	Drinkable
Aquifer	Underground layer of rock that holds water
Groundwater	Water that is under the ground

Social Studies Vocabulary	Meaning
Rural	Land outside of a city; country
Subsistence farming	Growing just enough crops to survive, without surplus food
Prime minister	The chief executive in parliamentary governments
Parliament	A national legislative body
Developing countries	Countries that have little wealth
Infrastructure	Public services and systems

Try It

Read the passage. Think about the meaning of the highlighted words. Use the questions to help you.

The Great Famine

During the 19th century, Ireland was a largely rural country. Ireland was governed by Great Britain at the time. The rural Irish often lived on small subsistence farms on subdivided land that was leased from absentee landlords. They got most of their nutrition from just one food. That food was the potato.

> **What do you think an *absentee landlord* is?**

Originally brought to Europe from South America by the Spanish, the potato took time to catch on in most of Europe. But in Ireland, the potato quickly became a vital source of nutrition. In fact, the Irish of the early 19th century were said to eat an average of between five and eight pounds of potatoes a day! The potato had many advantages, since it contains many vitamins and minerals. Unfortunately, the potato crop could fail. A potato blight might wreck an entire season's crop in one region, and the people there would go hungry. This happened several times, but it was not until 1845 that a potato blight spread and destroyed as much as one half of the country's crop. This particular blight was a fungus-like microorganism called *Phytophthora infestans.* In 1846, the blight destroyed three-fourths of the country's potatoes, and Ireland's poor began to starve.

> **Where could you look to find the meaning of the word *blight*?**

In England, the prime minister and parliament argued about what to do. In 1845, the prime minister, Sir Robert Peel, arranged for corn and corn meal to be sent from the United States to Ireland, where it was sold. Unfortunately, both foods required complicated processing or cooking in order to become edible. In 1846, the British arranged for a public works program to be set up in Ireland to help the starving poor. However, Sir Charles Trevelyan, the man who was in charge of overseeing the program, believed that the "judgment of God sent the calamity to teach the Irish a lesson." Starving employees were paid very low wages to do back-breaking jobs such as digging ditches.

Eventually, soup kitchens were set up that fed some three million people. Unfortunately, they were closed in 1847. By around that time, historians say, "famine fatigue" took hold in England. Many English grew tired of hearing about the famine, and so stopped paying attention to the awful things that were happening. As the famine continued, estate owners started to evict the poor who could not pay their rent. Up to half a million people had to leave their homes.

> **Based on context, can you determine the meaning of *evict*?**

Continued on the next page ▶

Continued from the previous page

Charity came from unexpected places. First, Calcutta gave a substantial amount. Then, in 1845, the leader of the Ottoman Empire, Sultan Abdülmecid, stated that he would donate 10,000 pounds to relief efforts in Ireland. However Queen Victoria asked that he send only one thousand. (She had contributed only two thousand pounds.) The sultan eventually gave the country one thousand pounds worth of silver, and sent three ships full of food. The Choctaw sent $710, just a few years after they were forced from their own homes in the southeastern United States.

Shockingly, during the famine's worst years, grain and cattle were being shipped out of Ireland to England. Yet Ireland's poor had no access to this food. Historians estimate that roughly one million Irish died during the famine, from starvation and other diseases. Perhaps another two million people emigrated to the United States, Canada, and Australia in the late 1840s and the decade that followed.

What does the word *emigrated* mean?

Why do writers sometimes have to use academic vocabulary?

Apply It

Read the passage. Answer the questions on the next page.

Water Watch

What should we do about water? While today most people in the United States have all the drinking water that they need, a time may be coming when we will need to be much more careful. Certain areas of the country have already faced prolonged drought, forcing local governments and industries to review their water management. A vast quantity of this precious natural resource, which we need to survive, is being used in industry today to create everything from flat screen televisions to books.

In many developing countries, there are people who still have to wait hours in line to get the water they need. And they sometimes have to carry it home over great distances. In fact, one out of six people in the world does not have access to plentiful and cheap, clean water. In India, where good access to inexpensive water was common in urban areas thirty years ago, acquiring water has become a major source of aggravation to people of all classes.

The problem, apparently, isn't that we do not have enough water for everyone to drink. It's that many people around the world do not have access to relatively *pure* water. Water-borne illnesses can be deadly, and water often needs to be treated before it is potable. Transporting the treated water from a treatment plant to a consumer can be expensive and difficult.

Clean water is contaminated by pollutants from industry and from traces of the medicines people use. These pollutants can harm the fish that live in the water, and may have other unforeseen environmental and health effects.

Drinking water is not the only area of concern. Our water use can affect the world around us. When people need water for farming or industry in relatively dry areas, they use groundwater. Often it is used faster than it can be replaced. That means that the ecosystems in these regions will change. Animals and plants that once could survive in a relatively dry environment by taking advantage of aquifers and groundwater are no longer able to do so.

Continued on the next page ➤

Continued from the previous page

According to Charles Fishman, the author of *The Big Thirst*, the average United States citizen uses an average of 99 gallons of water a day for drinking, washing, and flushing toilets. On top of that, the average American requires an average of 250 gallons of water to power their household heating or air conditioning systems.

New technologies and new ways of thinking about water can help in the water dilemma. Instead of using water that has been treated for drinking to water plants and lawns, water systems could use so-called "gray water" for these purposes. This is water that hasn't been purified to the standards for drinking water, but is still relatively clean. Old infrastructure also needs to be updated. Fishman writes that we lose one out of six gallons of treated water before it reaches our faucets. One gallon of water is lost through leaks in the system.

Use "Water Watch" to answer the questions. Write your answers in complete sentences.

1. How is water a *natural resource*?

_____

_____

2. What are *developing countries*?

_____

_____

3. If water is *potable*, what can you do with it?

_____

_____

4. What is *groundwater*?

_____

_____

5. What is an *aquifer*?

_____

_____

6. What does the word *infrastructure* mean?

_____

_____

Graphic Organizers

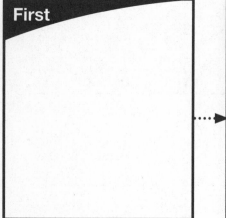 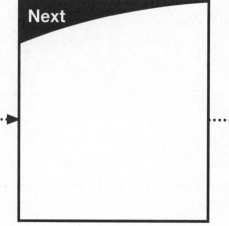 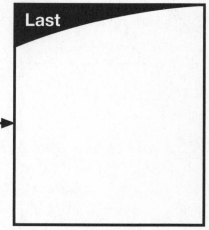

First → **Next** → **Last**

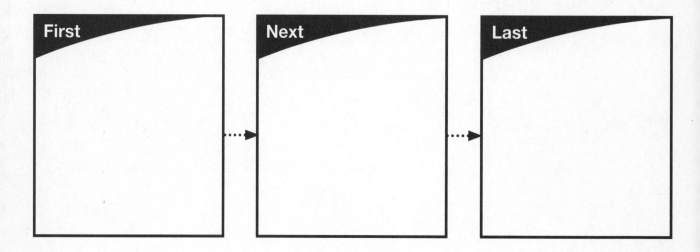

First → **Next** → **Last**

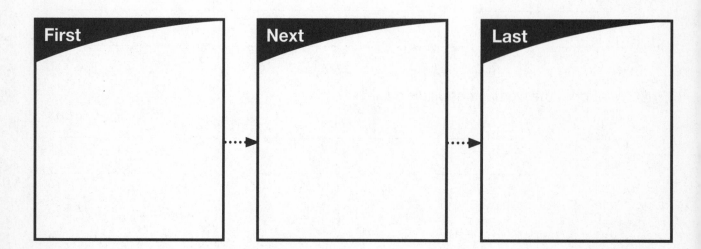

First → **Next** → **Last**

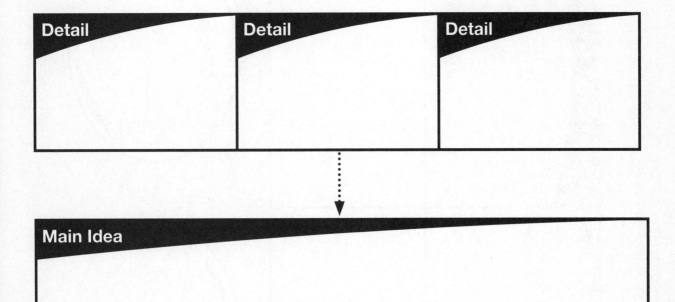

Detail

Detail

Detail

Main Idea

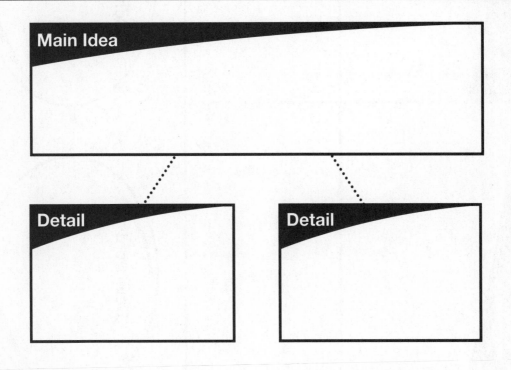

Main Idea

Detail

Detail

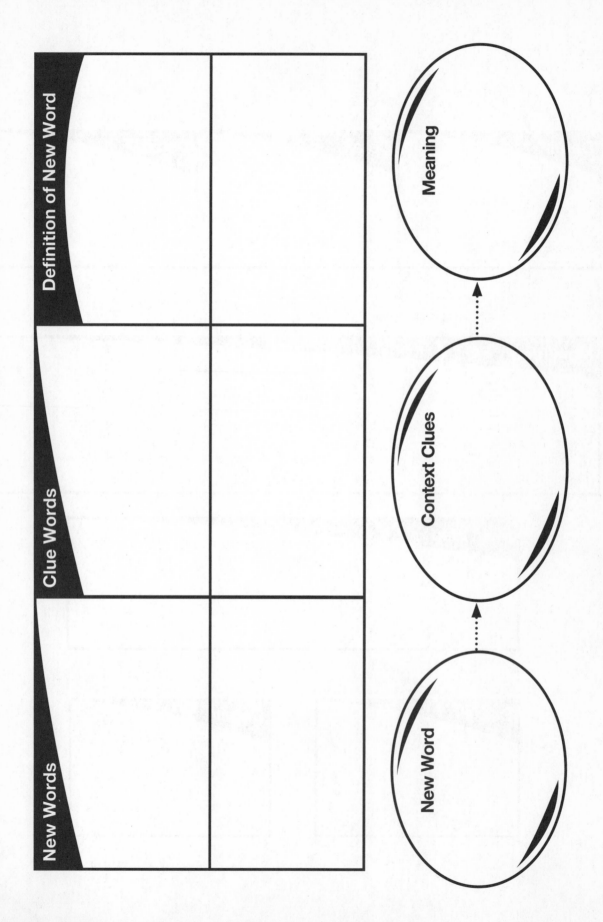

New Words	Clue Words	Definition of New Word

New Word → **Context Clues** → **Meaning**

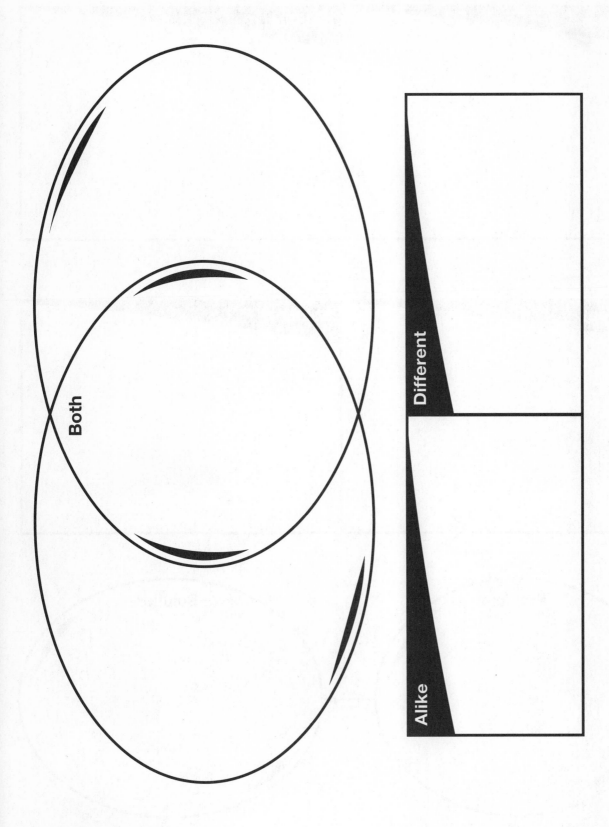

Both

Different

Alike

Problem	Solution

Problem	Solution

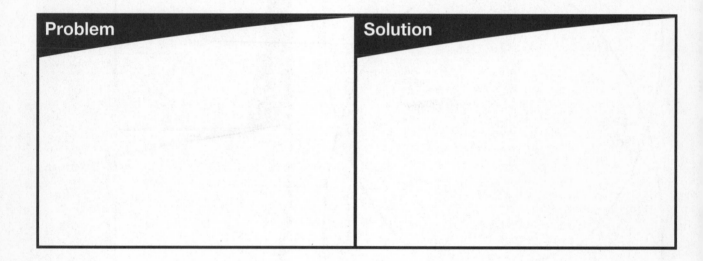

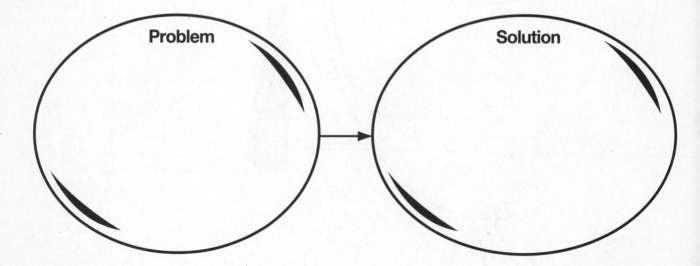